D1285105

CAPTURED

Linda Barr

SADDLEBACK
EDUCATIONAL PUBLISHING

ASTONISHING HEADLINES

SADDLEBACK
EDUCATIONAL PUBLISHING
www.sdlback.com

ISBN-13: 978-1-61651-919-3
ISBN-10: 1-61651-919-3
eBook: 978-1-61247-076-4

Printed in Guangzhou, China
0712/CA21201055

17 16 15 14 13   1 2 3 4 5

Photo Credits: page 11, Picture History; page 23, Reuters Photo Archive; page 49, Steve Helber, EPA Photos; page 66–67, Warrick Page / Getty Images News / Getty Images; pages 74–75, © Tourdottk | Dreamstime.com; page 86, Boston Globe / Boston Globe / Getty Images

CONTENTS

INTRODUCTION

A capture can be a triumph, an achievement, or a tragedy. It all depends on the reason for it. In this book, you will read about a runaway slave. He was recaptured just before the Civil War, and was returned to slavery. The debate over slavery tore our nation apart. It was an important time for our country.

Most people are captured because they have committed crimes. During World War II, the Nazis killed millions of people. After Germany lost the war, many Nazis went into hiding. However, their crimes could not be forgotten. People who lost family members wanted justice. Most of the surviving Nazis are now elderly, but they are still pursued—and captured.

Some criminals try to escape after they are captured. Most people thought Alcatraz prison escape-proof. Do you think anyone ever made it out? In Chapter 3, you will find out.

Do you remember the Washington, DC snipers? They killed 10 people and held millions hostage. You will read how the police, the FBI, and other groups captured these cold-blooded killers.

Many people thought Saddam Hussein would never be captured. They thought he was too powerful. Yet Saddam was captured without a shot being fired. You will learn how US troops finally found him.

In each chapter of this book, you will learn about an exciting and important capture!

Fugitive Slave Recaptured!
DATAFILE

Timeline

1850

Compromise of 1850 sets up the Fugitive Slave Act. Citizens must capture runaway slaves.

1861

The Civil War begins.

1865

The Civil War ends. Abraham Lincoln is shot. Slavery is abolished.

Where are Virginia and Boston?

Key Terms

free state—a state that outlawed slavery

fugitive—someone who is running away

master—in the old South, the boss of slaves

slave—a person made to work against his or her will; a person who is owned by another

slave state—a state that allowed slavery

?

Did You Know?

The Mason-Dixon Line was the boundary between Maryland and Pennsylvania. It, along with the Ohio River, was thought of as the dividing line between the slave states south of it and the free states north of it. Washington, DC, was in the South. Until 1850, Washington, DC, allowed slavery.

Fugitive Slave Recaptured!

The Runaway

Anthony Burns was born as a slave in 1834. However, he was allowed more freedom than most. For example, he could work for other people. He just had to pay his master part of what he earned. Still, Burns wanted to be truly free.

In 1854, Burns worked in Richmond, Virginia. He heard about freedom in the North, so he boarded a ship headed for Boston. He ran away from his master, Charles Suttle.

When Burns arrived in Boston, he sent a letter back to his brother, who was also Suttle's slave.

Suttle found and read the letter. Now he knew where Burns had gone. Suttle was determined to get him back.

Back then, Americans had strong—and different—feelings about slavery. Many in the South thought they had a right to own slaves. They needed slaves to work on their large farms. Many in the North believed that slavery was wrong. As more states joined the nation, Congress tried to keep an equal number of free and slave states.

In 1850, California wanted to join the nation. It chose to be a free state. To balance this, Congress compromised. It passed the Fugitive Slave Act. This act said that everyone had to help catch runaway slaves. That even included Northerners.

The Fugitive Slave Act helped Suttle. It required the people of Boston to help him catch Anthony Burns.

Captured!

Like Burns, many slaves fled to the North. Other African Americans living in the North had never been slaves. Yet they were all being hunted down and sent to the South. Many African Americans escaped to Canada. They were not safe anywhere in the United States.

Using the Fugitive Slave Act, Charles Suttle had Burns arrested. The date was May 24, 1854. The arrest shocked the people of Boston.

Burns was held in the federal courthouse. About 2,000 angry people gathered there. They wanted to free Burns. Some charged the heavily guarded building. A deputy was stabbed and died. Still, Burns was not freed. In fact, President Franklin Pierce sent Marines to make sure Burns did not get away.

CAUTION!!
COLORED PEOPLE
OF BOSTON, ONE & ALL,

You are hereby respectfully CAUTIONED and advised, to avoid conversing with the

Watchmen and Police Officers of Boston,

For since the recent ORDER OF THE MAYOR & ALDERMEN, they are empowered to act as

KIDNAPPERS
AND
Slave Catchers,

And they have already been actually employed in KIDNAPPING, CATCHING, AND KEEPING SLAVES. Therefore, if you value your LIBERTY, and the *Welfare of the Fugitives* among you, *Shun* them in every possible manner, as so many *HOUNDS* on the track of the most unfortunate of your race.

Keep a Sharp Look Out for KIDNAPPERS, and have TOP EYE open.

APRIL 24, 1851.

This poster warns African Americans to avoid talking to watchmen and police officers in Boston. After Congress passed the Fugitive Slave Act, African Americans could be seized and sent south into slavery without a fair trial.

Convicted!

On June 2, 1854, a court convicted Burns of being a fugitive slave. That day, he was bound with chains and forced to march from the courthouse to a ship that would take him back to Virginia. About 50,000 people lined the streets of Boston to watch Burns pass. Many yelled, "Shame! Shame!" at the 2,000 troops guarding Burns. The soldiers had orders to fire upon the crowd if anyone tried to free Burns. That day, he was shipped back to Charles Suttle.

It took an African American church a year to raise enough money to buy Burns' freedom. The cost was $1,300, which was a great deal of money then.

Within a year, Burns was back in Boston. Now he was truly free. He attended Oberlin College for two years. Later, he moved to Canada. Burns became a pastor. In poor health all his life, he died at age 28.

Burns was the last fugitive slave to be recaptured in Massachusetts. Of course, his release was not the end of the story. Slavery was still legal. But the Fugitive Slave Act actually helped end slavery. It forced Northerners to participate in the recapture of runaway slaves. Now slavery affected them, too. As a result, many more Northerners decided to work against slavery. Tensions between the North and the South grew. The nation would be united again only after a bloody civil war.

Adolf Eichmann Captured!
DATAFILE

Timeline

1944

Adolf Eichmann reports to Hitler that 6 million Jews have been killed.

1945

World War II ends.

1960

Eichmann is captured in Argentina.

Where is Argentina?

Key Terms

Avengers—a group that hunts Nazi criminals and brings them to justice

concentration camp—a Nazi prison where many people were tortured and killed; death camp

Gestapo—the German secret police

ghetto—a part of a city where a minority group is forced to live

Mossad—an Israeli spy group

safe house—a secret hiding place

Did You Know?

Nazis are still fleeing justice. Nazi Maurice Papon was convicted of sending 1,500 Jews to death camps. In 1999 at age 89, he escaped from French authorities.

Adolf Eichmann Captured!

Proud but Hiding

During World War II, Adolf Eichmann was part of the German Gestapo. It was his idea to collect Jewish people. He herded them into ghettos. Later, he was proud of his role in killing six million Jews.

Before the war, Eichmann tried to become an engineer, but he failed. Still, he was good at organizing things. In 1932, he joined the Nazi Party. There he quickly gained power. By 1941, he was creating death camps. They were the "final solution" to the Jewish "problem."

The war ended in 1945. Germany and Japan lost. Many Nazi leaders were captured and put on trial. Many others escaped. They went into hiding. Eichmann was one of them.

The Hunters

A group called the Avengers formed. It hunted down more than 1,000 Nazis. Still, the Avengers could not find Eichmann. He stayed in Europe until 1950. Then he escaped to Argentina. His wife and children followed him in 1952.

In 1957, the Mossad learned that Eichmann was in Argentina. In Argentina, Eichmann's son found a girlfriend. But he did not know that she was Jewish. The son boasted about his father. He was proud of his dad's role in killing millions of Jews. The son wished that the Nazis had "finished the job."

The Mossad learned where the son lived. They rushed to the Eichmanns' home, but the family was gone.

The Mossad continued to hunt Eichmann. They were worried about catching the right man. All they had were blurred pictures of him. He had left behind no fingerprints. All of the German secret police had a tattoo. However, Eichmann had his tattoo removed.

In 1959, the Mossad learned that Eichmann had changed his name. Now he called himself Ricardo Klement. However, his son kept his old name. The Mossad traced the son to a house in Buenos Aires. At the house, they saw a man who might be Eichmann, but they were not sure.

Then on March 21, 1960, the Mossad watched "Klement" give his wife a bouquet of flowers. Now they were sure. That date was the Eichmanns' silver wedding anniversary.

Captured!

More than 30 Mossad members prepared for the capture. Some of them had suffered in the concentration camps, and many had lost family members in the camps. One man had been part of the Avengers.

The Mossad kept its plans secret from the Argentine police. They knew that the police would think the capture was a kidnapping.

By May 11, 1960, the Mossad was ready. They would catch Eichmann when he returned from work at about 7:40 p.m. They waited outside his house. Two sets of men pretended to fix their cars. They waited as three buses stopped, one by one. Eichmann was not on any of them. Had they missed him?

Finally, a fourth bus stopped. There he was! The agents grabbed Eichmann. They stuffed him in a car where they gagged him and tied him up. Soon they had him back at their safe house. At first, Eichmann denied who he really was, but then he became frightened and nervous. Suddenly, Eichmann was eager to tell all he knew.

The Mossad members were amazed at how ordinary Eichmann seemed. Here was a man who had ordered the deaths of millions of innocent people. Now he just seemed pitiful.

A flight from Argentina to Israel was scheduled on May 20. The Mossad waited until then. If it left earlier than scheduled, the police or government officials might become suspicious.

Justice at Last

After his capture, Eichmann's family looked for him, but they could not call the police. Their Nazi friends were afraid to help because the Mossad was looking for them, too.

To get Eichmann out of the country, the Mossad had a plan. An agent pretended to have an accident. He was taken to the hospital with "brain damage." The agent "recovered" and planned to fly to Israel on May 20. Actually, Eichmann took his place on the plane.

On May 20, the Mossad drugged Eichmann to keep him quiet. At the airport, the agents told the guards that their friend was sleeping because he drank too much. Soon Eichmann was in the plane and on his way to Israel.

In 1961, Eichmann finally stood trial for his war crimes. The trial took place in Israel and lasted from April 2 until August 14. The world closely watched the trial. During the trial, Eichmann sat in a bulletproof glass box. As his terrible deeds were described, people shouted and cried. Some wanted to kill him.

In the end, Eichmann asked for mercy. He begged for understanding. After all, he had only been following orders. The death camps were the fault of the Nazi government.

Eichmann was convicted, sentenced to death, and hanged. The Jewish people were no longer defenseless. They now had their own nation and their own army. They had forced Eichmann to answer for his crimes and his cruelty.

Adolf Eichmann stands trial for his crimes in Israel.

Prisoners in Alcatraz: Captured or Escaped?

DATAFILE

Timeline

1946
Bernard Coy and five others try to escape.

1962
Inmates Frank Lee Morris and two brothers escape ... maybe.

1963
Alcatraz Prison closes after 29 years.

Where is Alcatraz Island?

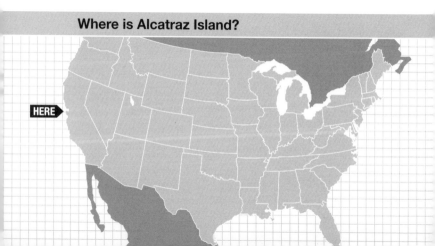

HERE

Key Terms

boarding school—a place where students live while they attend school

hostage—someone taken by force to pressure someone else

hostiles—a term used long ago to identify groups of Native Americans who resisted government orders

inmate—a prisoner

privilege—a favor that is granted to someone

vent—an opening for air

warden—the person in charge of a prison

Did You Know?

Alcatraz Island is now one of San Francisco's most popular tourist attractions. More than one million tourists visit every year, coming from all over the world.

Prisoners in Alcatraz: Captured or Escaped?

In the Beginning

Alcatraz was once a bare, rocky island in San Francisco Bay. In 1853, the US Army built a fort on this island. It had a lighthouse. The fort was meant to defend California. However, its cannons were fired at a ship only once. They missed.

By 1861, the island was used as a prison. First, it held Civil War prisoners. In 1898, it held prisoners from the Spanish-American War.

In 1906, a huge earthquake shook San Francisco. Many jails were destroyed. Their prisoners were sent to the island. In 1912, a cellhouse was built.

It was three stories high. By the late 1920s, nearly all the cells were full. The prison became known as "The Rock."

Alcatraz was used as a prison for 29 years. To the inmates, freedom seemed so close. After all, they could see San Francisco just across the bay. The guards patrolled the bay in boats to watch for escapees. Few prisoners tried to leave by swimming. The water there rarely gets warmer than 55 degrees. Fast currents make the trip even harder.

Still, 34 prisoners risked their lives to get away, including two who tried to escape twice. Nearly all of these men were killed or recaptured. A few are still missing. Two groups almost made it. Inmates Bernard Coy and Paul Cretzer led one group. The other group included inmates Frank Lee Morris and brothers Clarence and John Anglin.

The Battle of Alcatraz

Most prisoners at Alcatraz were violent and dangerous. They had been sent there from other prisons. Many had refused to follow prison rules. Some had tried to escape.

At Alcatraz, prisoners had four rights. They could have food, clothing, shelter, and medical care. Everything else was a privilege. Inmates had to work to gain privileges. One privilege was a visit from family members. Another was having a job in the prison.

It took most inmates five years to prove they could be trusted. Only then were they sent to another prison. Some inmates did not wait. They decided to escape. Two of them were Bernard Coy and Paul Cretzer.

Coy had robbed a bank in Kentucky. He arrived at Alcatraz in 1937. Cretzer had robbed three banks.

He had also escaped from another prison and killed a US marshal. He was sent to Alcatraz in 1944.

By 1946, Coy and Cretzer had a plan. They invited four other inmates in on it. They would steal guns and blast their way out of the prison.

Coy did manage to get some guns. He also released 24 other convicts from their cells. However, he could not get the key that would let them into the prison recreation yard. Desperate, the gang took nine guards hostage. They pushed the guards into two cells. The Battle of Alcatraz had begun.

Call the Marines!

The prison warden alerted the marines, the navy, and the Coast Guard. The marines rushed the island and bombarded the cellhouse with mortars and grenades. Navy and Coast Guard boats ringed the island. Thousands of people stood on the San Francisco shore and watched. They heard gunfire from the prison.

Many inmates were trapped inside. They were not trying to escape, but they were in great danger. Some hid behind mattresses.

Bullets flew, and the army threw grenades into the cellblock every half-hour. In time, Coy, Cretzer, and the rest of the gang knew they could not escape, but they decided not to give up. They would fight it out.

Cretzer knew that the hostages could identify him, so he opened fire on them, hitting several. They lay on the cell floor for 10 hours, bleeding. At least one of the guards pretended to be dead, and one did die later.

The fighting lasted two days. Finally, Coy, Cretzer, and another gang member were shot and killed. The other three gang members returned to their cells. They tried to pretend they were not part of the escape attempt. However, all three were caught. Two were executed in 1948. The third one had 99 years added to his prison term.

During the fighting, two guards were killed. At least 18 people were injured. None of the six inmates escaped.

The Great Escape!

Did you see the movie *Escape from Alcatraz*? It starred Clint Eastwood. If you did, you know about Frank Lee Morris and the Anglin brothers. Morris had been in and out of prison his whole life. His first conviction came when he was only 13. His crimes included armed robbery. He was sent to Alcatraz in 1960, after escaping from other prisons.

John and Clarence Anglin were bank robbers. They, too, had a history of escaping from prison. Another inmate, Allan West, helped in the "great escape." He had been sent to Alcatraz twice. West might have planned the whole escape. However, he was not able to leave with the other three inmates.

The four inmates prepared for their escape for seven months. First, they stole tools and supplies. Then they made a raft and life preservers out of more than 50 raincoats and glue. They also made lifelike heads and added human hair from the prison barbershop. They would leave the heads behind in their bunks, along with rolled-up blankets. They hoped the guards would think the inmates were still in their beds.

The inmates also tried using homemade drills to make their cell vent holes larger. However, the drills were too noisy. The men did most of the digging by hand. They also made fake walls to hide their work.

By June 11, 1962, the four inmates were ready for their escape.

Success?

The men planned to leave right after lights-out at 9:30 p.m. Three of them escaped from their cells through their vent holes, but West had trouble pulling his vent out of its hole. Morris and the two brothers climbed up pipes to the cellhouse roof, crossed the roof, and climbed down more pipes to the shower area.

No one ever saw the three men again. By the time West got his vent out, the others were gone.

Later, West explained their plan. They were going to use the raft to get to nearby Angel Island. There they would rest and then swim to the coast. After they stole a car and clothes, the four inmates would go their separate ways.

Did Morris and the brothers really escape from Alcatraz? No one is sure, but the FBI thinks their plan failed. No car or clothing robberies were reported for 12 days after the escape. Two life vests were found floating in the bay. Also, police found a package of letters and photographs belonging to the brothers. They were tightly wrapped to keep them dry.

Several weeks later, a body in a blue uniform was found near the coast. The clothing looked like a prison uniform. However, the body could not be identified. It had been in the water too long.

The three inmates are still missing and presumed drowned. They would have been better off if they had stayed captured!

Alcatraz—The Rock—in San Francisco Bay

Hopi Inmates at Alcatraz

Not only convicts were kept at Alcatraz. Native Americans were sent there, too. The largest group was 19 Hopi "hostiles." These men were sent to prison in 1895. What was their crime? The US government tried to force the Hopis to leave their land. They wanted to give the Hopis new land to farm. The Hopis refused to farm the land that was assigned to them. They—and other Hopis—also would not send their children to government boarding schools.

In fact, the government tried to erase the Hopi language and culture. For example, children at the boarding schools were beaten if they spoke the Hopi language.

So the 19 Hopi "hostiles" were arrested. They were sent to Alcatraz.

The San Francisco newspaper called them "nineteen murderous-looking Apache Indians." Of course, they were Hopis—and not violent at all. The article said the men "are prisoners and prisoners they shall stay until they have learned to appreciate the advantage of education."

The men were kept in tiny wooden cells. Two of them missed the births of their children. The babies died before their fathers could see them.

These Hopis were supposed to perform hard labor until they saw "the error of their evil ways." They were jailed from January 3 until August 7, 1895. After they promised to obey all orders, they were released.

CHAPTER 4

Washington, DC, Snipers Captured!
DATAFILE

Timeline

October 2–22, 2002

Unknown snipers kill 10 people and wound three others in the DC area.

October 24, 2002

Snipers Muhammad and Malvo are arrested.

Where were the shootings?

Key Terms

frenzy—great panic or excitement; madness

sniper—someone who hides and shoots at others

tarot card—a card used to tell fortunes

witness—someone who sees something taking place

wound—to injure

? Did You Know?

The police and FBI caught the Washington, DC snipers in just 22 days, despite many wrong turns.

Washington, DC, Snipers Captured!

The Shootings Begin

On October 2, 2002, a bullet went through a window at a craft store in Montgomery County, Maryland. It was 5:20 p.m. No one was hurt, and few people paid much attention. No one knew what was coming next—except for two killers.

Less than an hour later, they shot and killed a man in a grocery store parking lot not far from the craft store. At 7:41 the next morning, they shot and killed another man while he mowed some grass. Soon afterward, they shot and killed a cab driver at a gas station. By that evening, three more people had been shot. In all, the killers shot and killed five people on October 3.

By then, the local police were in a frenzy. They knew they had one or more snipers on their hands and had begun to search for them. That same day, the DC police stopped a blue Chevy Caprice for a minor problem. They talked to the driver and his passenger. They also checked the car's license tag. They had no reason to keep the men, so they let them continue on their way.

Two hours later, a witness to the last murder of that day remembered something. The witness had seen a dark-colored Caprice leaving the scene. Police started looking for the car. However, the report was too late. The snipers selected their next victim.

Clue from the Killers

The next afternoon, October 4, they shot and wounded a woman in the parking lot of a craft store in Virginia, 50 miles south of Washington, DC.

On October 7 at 8:09 a.m., they shot and wounded a 13-year-old boy. His aunt had just dropped him off at his middle school in Maryland, not far from Washington, DC. This time, the killers left a tarot card behind. Written on it was this message: "Mister Policeman, I am God." Police also located the matted grass where the shooter had lain in wait for the victim. There, they found a shell casing from the gun. Both the woman and the boy were lucky. They survived.

The next day, the police found one of the killers, but they did not know it. A Baltimore officer spotted him asleep in his car. It was parked outside a sandwich shop. The officer checked the car's New Jersey plates. He also checked the man's Washington State driver's license. They were both in order. The killer said he was on his way to see his father. After asking for directions, he drove away.

On the evening of October 9, they shot and killed a man while he filled his car at a gas station in Manassas, Virginia. Two days later, they shot and killed a father of six. He had also been filling his car at a Virginia gas station.

More Twists, More Deaths

The police and FBI formed a task force. However, they no longer looked for a Caprice. Witnesses said they saw a white van at the crime scenes. The task force searched for that van.

On October 14, they shot and killed an FBI analyst in the parking garage of a hardware store in Falls Church, Virginia. Some witnesses saw a

Caprice fleeing the scene. A man named Matthew Dowdy reported seeing a cream-colored van.

On October 18, Dowdy was arrested. He admitted that he had filed a false report. He had not seen a van leaving the hardware store. False tips like this one made the task force's job even more difficult.

Also on October 18, one of the killers called a priest in Ashland, Virginia. The killer again claimed to be God. He also mentioned crimes in Alabama. Thinking the call was a prank, the priest hung up. He did not report the call to the police.

On October 19, they shot and wounded a man in a parking lot in Ashland. This time, the killers left behind a letter. It demanded $10 million to stop the shootings. The letter also said the killers had made five calls, including one to the FBI and a priest in Ashland. They complained that no one listened to them. Now they warned, "Your children are not safe anywhere at any time."

Police Close In

On October 20, the police found the Ashland priest. He told them about the call. He remembered that the killer had mentioned crimes in Alabama. The task force thought this might be a clue. They called the police in Montgomery, Alabama. Yes, this town had a shooting much like those in the Washington area. On September 21, 2002, a gunman or gunmen shot two women outside a store. One had died.

The next day, members of the task force flew to Alabama. They were given a fingerprint. Soon they had a name: Lee Boyd Malvo. He was wanted by the Immigration and Naturalization Service (INS). His INS file mentioned a friend named John Muhammad.

The same day, a man called the Virginia police, claiming to be the sniper. The police traced the call to a gas station. There, officers found a white minivan. They quickly arrested the two men inside. They were illegal immigrants, but not the snipers.

The next day, October 22, the snipers shot and killed a bus driver in his bus.

That day, the task force learned that Malvo had lived in Tacoma, Washington. On October 23, they flew there. In Malvo's former backyard was a tree stump. He had used it for target practice. The bullet fragments in the stump matched those in the shootings!

Soon police linked Muhammad to the Caprice that the police had stopped on October 8. Now everyone searched for the Caprice.

Captured!

On October 24, police and the FBI captured both killers. They were found asleep in the Caprice, parked at a rest stop near Frederick, Maryland. In the car was the rifle used in the shootings. The trunk of the car had a hole in it. The hole allowed the killers to lie in the trunk and shoot without being seen.

In December 2003, the killers were brought to trial in Virginia. Muhammad was convicted of one murder. He was given the death sentence. Malvo, 17 years old during the shootings, claimed insanity. His lawyer said that Muhammad, age 42, had brainwashed Malvo. Still, the jury convicted Malvo of one murder. He was sentenced to life in prison. In a second trial in 2004, Malvo was convicted of one murder and one attempted murder.

Malvo and Muhammad killed 10 people in the Washington, DC area. They might have killed four more in other states. They also wounded at least three people. The two men kept millions living in fear.

The task force missed opportunities to capture the men. Still, in only 22 days, they found a number of clues. These clues led them to the killers.

Now the killers were behind bars. People living in the Washington, DC area could relax at last. Parents let their children play outside again. Gas station customers stopped looking over their shoulders. Business picked up at stores. The community—and the nation—stopped holding its breath.

John Allen Muhammad on trial for murder in the DC sniper shootings

Saddam Hussein Captured!
DATAFILE

Timeline

July 1979

Saddam Hussein becomes Iraqi dictator.

August 1990

Saddam invades Kuwait.

March 2003

Saddam's regime toppled.

December 2003

Saddam captured by US forces.

Where is Iraq?

HERE

Key Terms

Baath—a political party in Iraq

coup—a sudden attack to take over a government

Kurds—an ethnic group living in northern Iraq

peasant—a poor farmer or worker

regime—a government

Shiites—a religious group in Iraq; a member of a branch of Islam

Did You Know?

Hussein began his political career in 1958. His first act was to kill a supporter of the Iraqi leader who was in power.

CHAPTER 5

Saddam Hussein Captured!

Captured "Like a Rat"

US troops searched the farm by moonlight. They were outside Tikrit, north of Baghdad. They had already spent months trying to find Saddam Hussein. The ex-dictator of Iraq was well hidden.

The soldiers poked through a dirty two-room hut. One room had two beds, some books, and clothes. The other room was a messy kitchen. It was stacked with boxes of rotting oranges. Outside the hut, someone noticed a rug on the ground and pulled it back. Underneath, a thick piece of Styrofoam covered a deep, narrow hole. When the soldiers lifted off the Styrofoam, they heard noises coming from deep inside the hole. Then two dirty hands appeared, upraised.

Without firing a shot, US forces had captured Saddam Hussein like a rat in a hole!

At first, the soldiers thought they had found a peasant. Saddam was bearded and dressed in rags. He did not look like a powerful and brutal leader.

It was a surprising end for Saddam. He was born in 1937. As a student, he had joined Iraq's Baath Party. In 1968, Saddam helped plan the coup that brought the Baath Party to power. By 1979, Saddam was the dictator of Iraq. He used fear to control the 24 million Iraqis. Soon he was a leader in the Arab world.

In 1980, Saddam ordered his troops to attack Iran. The war lasted eight years. Hundreds of thousands of soldiers from both nations died. There was no clear winner.

Ruling with Fear

The Iraqis suffered under Saddam. In the late 1980s, the Kurds rose up against him. Saddam dealt with them brutally. Soon, about 180,000 Kurds were missing. Later, mass graves were found. He used nerve gas to kill another 5,000 Kurds.

August 2, 1990, Saddam attacked the tiny country of Kuwait. His forces tortured and killed hundreds of Kuwaitis. They set Kuwait's oil wells on fire. They fired missiles at Israel. They even fired them at Saudi Arabia.

In February 1991, the United Nations stepped in. Troops from the United States and other nations went to Kuwait. Four days later, the Gulf War was over. Saddam withdrew from Kuwait. The United Nations told him to destroy his weapons. He said he did.

Some Iraqis hoped this would be a good time to rebel against Saddam. They were wrong. His forces may have killed as many as 60,000 Shiites and Kurds toward the end of the Gulf War.

In 1992, Saddam drained the marshes in southern Iraq. This drove the people known as Marsh Arabs from their homes. Tens of thousands were arrested or killed. Many just disappeared.

Despite losing the war, Saddam still ruled Iraq. He trusted few people, not even his own family. In 1995, two of his sons-in-law fled to Jordan. Saddam asked them to come back and promised they would be safe. When they returned, he killed them.

Captured!

Then came September 11, 2001. Terrorists struck the United States. Two planes crashed into the World Trade Center. Another hit the Pentagon. A fourth crashed into a field in Pennsylvania. Osama bin Laden said his group were the attackers. He leads a group called al-Qaeda. Al-Qaeda was based in Afghanistan. The Afghan government protected them.

President George W. Bush sent troops to Afghanistan. After some fighting, a new government took over. It no longer protected al-Qaeda. The terrorists fled to other nations.

Some US leaders thought Saddam helped with the 9/11 attacks. President Bush decided to go to war against Iraq. He believed that Saddam had not destroyed his weapons. He thought Saddam would use those weapons against us.

US soldiers invaded Iraq on March 20, 2003. Within three weeks, they defeated the Baath troops, and put the Baath Party out of power. Saddam went into hiding. Over the next months, US forces searched for him. On December 13, Operation Red Dawn began. About 600 troops took part in the raid. They learned that Saddam was hiding near a farm.

The troops searched the farm for Saddam. At first, they did not find him, but then they noticed the rug on the ground.

When they pulled Saddam out of his "spider hole," he was confused. He had a pistol in the hole, but he did not try to fire it. He also had $750,000 in US money.

Saddam on Trial

Saddam spoke to the US soldiers in English. "I am Saddam Hussein," he said. "I am president of Iraq. I want to negotiate."

The soldiers told him, "President Bush sends his regards."

Right after his capture, Saddam was cooperative and talkative. A short time later, however, he was defiant. Iraqi leaders met with him. They told him people were dancing in the streets, celebrating his capture. "Those are mobs," Saddam said.

The leaders asked him to explain the mass graves filled with his victims. "Those are thieves," Saddam insisted.

Saddam was asked about the killing of thousands of Kurds in 1988. He shrugged and said he had heard about it.

Saddam was tried in an Iraqi court. He still insisted that he was president of Iraq. Eleven of his supporters were also to be tried. Their lawyers said they could not receive a fair trial in Iraq. Security for the trial was a problem.

On November 5, 2006, Saddam Hussein was sentenced to death by hanging. On December 26 his appeal was rejected. He was executed on December 30, 2006.

The Kurds, Shiites, and other groups in Iraq do not get along well. For the good of their nation, they must find ways to work together.

Osama bin Laden
DATAFILE

Timeline

1993
Bin Laden forms militant Muslim group al Qaeda.

September 11, 2001
Four commercial planes are hijacked and used to attack significant locations in the United States.

May 2, 2011
Bin Laden is killed by US Navy SEALS in Abbottabad, Pakistan.

Where is Pakistan?

Key Terms

commercial plane—aircraft used to carry cargo or passengers for payment

compound—an area enclosed by a fence

talons—claws, especially belonging to a bird of prey

trident—a three-pronged spear

Did You Know?

SEAL stands for sea-air-land teams. The US Navy SEALs were created by President Kennedy in 1962 as an elite part of the US Navy. There are eight SEAL teams: 1, 2, 3, 4, 5, 7, 8, and 10. Our government does not acknowledge the existence of the elite of the elite, team 6.

CHAPTER 6

Osama bin Laden

Bin Laden is Dead

It was all over. The man who planned the destruction of the World Trade Center was dead.

On May 2, 2011, US Navy SEALs stormed Osama bin Laden's compound in Pakistan. In the middle of the night, the soldiers arrived in helicopters. They forced their way into the compound. They found bin Laden and shot him. He had been avoiding capture for nearly ten years.

The Central Intelligence Agency (CIA) had been spying on bin Laden's compound. They were tracking his messenger, Abu Ahmed al-Kuwaiti. Through this man, the CIA found bin Laden.

The compound was near Abbottabad in northeastern Pakistan. The three-story concrete building was less than a mile from a military school.

Concrete walls 12 to 18 feet high surrounded the compound. Barbed wire topped the walls. The third-floor balcony had a seven-foot privacy wall. It was tall enough for bin Laden to hide behind. He was six feet four inches tall.

The mission to find bin Laden was called Operation Neptune Spear. Neptune was the Roman god of the sea. He was often shown holding a trident, or three-pronged spear. It was a symbol of his power. Today's Navy SEAL gold badge features that same symbol. An American bald eagle grasps the trident in its talons.

The SEALs are specially trained warriors. Navy SEAL training is extremely tough. About two thirds of those attempting it drop out. SEALs take on special assignments—difficult, dangerous missions. So when President Barack Obama needed the best, he sent for the SEALs.

Al-Qaeda terrorist Osama bin Laden had been in hiding for nearly ten years. It had been that long since the attacks of September 11, 2001. Bin Laden was the mastermind behind those attacks. They were the worst ever on US soil.

Four planes were hijacked and used as missiles. One was flown into the Pentagon. Another crashed into a field in Pennsylvania.

The other two hijacked planes were flown into the World Trade Center towers. The Twin Towers had been, at one time, the tallest buildings in the world. Both towers caught fire and quickly collapsed to the ground. All told, nearly 3,000 people were killed.

After ten years in hiding, it was time to bring bin Laden to justice.

Once the CIA found bin Laden's compound in Pakistan, planning began. The CIA used satellite images to see the layout. They looked at old Google Earth images and found out the compound was built in 2004.

Other government agencies were involved in the operation too. They built a three-dimensional model of the building. And they figured out how many people were inside.

Including bin Laden, there were 22 people in the building when the SEALs landed. Five adults were killed: bin Laden, three other men, and one woman. Surviving were four women and 13 children.

After he was shot, bin Laden's body was removed from the compound. DNA testing proved his identity. There was other evidence as well. One of bin Laden's wives called out his name during the raid. Later, al-Qaeda confirmed that the body was in fact bin Laden's.

Locals and media gather outside the compound where Osama bin Laden was killed in an operation by US Navy Seals in Abottabad, Pakistan. Bin Laden was killed during a US military mission on May 2, 2011, at the compound.

Within 24 hours of his death, bin Laden was buried at sea. Following Muslim tradition, the body was washed. Then it was wrapped in a sheet. Last, it was placed onto a board that was tilted. Osama bin Laden's body slipped into the ocean.

The CIA gave the reason why bin Laden was buried at sea. If he had been buried on land, people could make a shrine. They could make him into a hero. That would not be proper for this terrorist who was responsible for killing so many people.

However, there are some things about the capture that bothered some people. The public was never shown photos or video of bin Laden's dead body. And no other hard evidence of his death was released to the public. This has caused a controversy.

Reporters from the Associated Press, or AP, have requested this information. So have other respected news organizations, such as CBS News. They have asked for copies of the DNA tests. The

Freedom of Information Act requires that the public be given this information. But so far the government has not provided it.

President Obama appeared on *60 Minutes* just two days after the raid. He confirmed that photos of bin Laden's dead body do exist. However, they are gruesome. "We don't trot this stuff out as trophies," the president said.

After the raid, people said Pakistan had sheltered bin Laden. The government of Pakistan denied this.

During the raid, the SEALs also seized a lot of computers, hard drives, and other data-holding materials. They were filled with valuable information about al-Qaeda's activities.

The raid was a big step toward shutting down al-Qaeda. Putting an end to terrorism will make the world a safer place.

Muammar al-Qaddafi
DATAFILE

Timeline

September 1969

At age twenty-seven, Muammar al-Qaddafi seizes control of Libya by military coup.

February 2011

Libyan protesters call for ouster of Qaddafi.

October 20, 2011

Libyan authorities announce Qaddafi's death near his home of Sirt, Libya.

Where is Libya?

HERE

Key Terms

autocrat—a ruler with supreme power

autopsy—an examination of a body after death to discover cause of death

demagogue—a leader who sways people with emotion

?

Did You Know?

Much of the country of Libya lies within the great Sahara Desert. Libya is larger than Alaska. It shares a border with Tunisia and Algeria in the west and Egypt to the east. The countries of Chad, Sudan, and Niger border Libya in the south.

Muammar al-Qaddafi

Qaddafi Falls from Power

Libya is an oil-rich country located west of Egypt in North Africa. It also borders Tunisia, Algeria, Niger, Chad, and Sudan.

Muammar al-Qaddafi was Libya's leader for many years. Seizing power from King Idris in 1969, Qaddafi and other military officers threw out Libya's constitution. They established a republic. However, it was clear that Qaddafi was the real leader. In 1977 he pretended to step down. But he actually remained Libya's head of state for 41 years.

During the 1970s he established relations with many dangerous politicians, such as Idi Amin. This former Ugandan dictator was known for his monstrous ways. The 2006 movie *The Last King of Scotland* is about Idi Amin.

Ronald Reagan called Qaddafi "the mad dog of the Middle East." During most of his reign, Libya was considered a pariah state. That's a country that is frowned upon by the rest of the world. (Pariah is another word for outcast.) It is a country that doesn't follow the same rules other countries do, especially rules on human rights.

Qaddafi also backed Mengistu Haile Mariam. This Ethiopian politician was charged with genocide. That's the killing of a large population of people. The Holocaust in World War II is an example of genocide. In 1977 and 1978, Mariam was responsible for the deaths of tens of thousands of Ethiopians.

Qaddafi was called an autocrat and a demagogue. An autocrat is a ruler with supreme power. A demagogue is a leader who sways people with emotion.

Muammar al-Qaddafi pictured on a huge billboard outside Tripoli, Libya, wearing a highly decorated and colorful

uniform and cap. Qaddafi images appeared throughout Libya. Most have now been vandalized and destroyed.

Qaddafi used his power to make his relatives fabulously wealthy. They lived in mansions and had American pop stars such as Beyoncé at their parties.

However, Qaddafi also did some good things for Libya. Under his reign, the literacy rate increased from 10 percent to over 80 percent. Libyans had the highest standard of living in Africa. This was due in large part to the money that Libya made from oil. Qaddafi kept oil operations running smoothly.

One of the bad things Qaddafi did was to forbid freedom of speech. We take that freedom for granted here in the United States. But in places like Libya, a person could be put to death for criticizing the ruler. Qaddafi even had people outside Libya executed.

Qaddafi also ordered an act of terrorism, the Lockerbie bombing. The Lockerbie bombing was in December 1988. A jumbo jet flying from London to New York blew up over Lockerbie, Scotland. The bombing killed 189 Americans and 43 British citizens. Some of the British citizens killed were on the ground. The plane destroyed their homes when it fell.

Twelve years later, a Libyan intelligence official was convicted of murder. After years of negotiations, Qaddafi arranged for $2.7 billion to be paid to the Lockerbie victims' families. After legal fees, each family got about $5.5 million.

In 2003, Libya admitted responsibility, but not guilt for the Lockerbie bombing.

In February 2011, civil war broke out in Libya. Rebels were trying to overthrow Qaddafi's government. They wanted him out. The rebel group is named the National Transitional Council (NTC). They said that the country was "shackled and enslaved under the feet of the tyrant Mu'ammar Gaddafi." Their army is called the National Liberation Army (NLA).

Protests in the city of Benghazi started the civil war. Benghazi is the second largest city in Libya after Tripoli. The protests in Benghazi spread throughout Libya. People were ready for a change.

Qaddafi and his family were based in Tripoli. They lived at the Bab al-Azizia, or "Splendid Gate." This elaborate compound was Qaddafi's central headquarters.

The compound featured a sculpture of a giant fist squeezing a US fighter jet. Qaddafi had the sculpture made because the United States bombed Libya in 1986. The sculpture symbolized Qaddafi's revenge.

When the rebels got close to Tripoli, Qaddafi's family fled to Algeria. He headed south to Libya's desert.

Rebels took over Bab al-Azizia on August 23,

2011. They sprayed graffiti over the base of the fist sculpture. Then they took it down and relocated it in the town of Misrata. It had become the symbol of Qaddafi.

Qaddafi was out of power. But he had a plan to overthrow the rebels. He was organizing his supporters in the Libyan desert. They were based in Sirte.

In October 2011, the rebels took Sirte. Qaddafi fled in a caravan. It had 75 vehicles in it, one behind the other. They were attempting to escape the rebels.

NATO aircraft—British, French, and American—fired on the convoy. Qaddafi escaped and hid in a drainage pipe. On October 20, 2011, Qaddafi was killed by the rebels. The autopsy showed he died from a bullet to the head.

CHAPTER 8

James "Whitey" Bulger

DATAFILE

Timeline

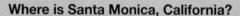

1943

A fourteen-year-old James Bulger is arrested for the first time.

1994

Bulger disappears before a court appearance.

June 22, 2011

James "Whitey" Bulger captured in Santa Monica, California.

Where is Santa Monica, California?

HERE

Key Terms

loan shark—a moneylender who charges extremely high interest rates

manhunt—an organized search for a person, especially a criminal

organized crime—a group of professional criminals who rely on crime as a way of life

?

Did You Know?

The Irish Mafia appeared in the United States in the early 19th century as Irish street gangs. The Irish Mafia gained power in Boston during Prohibition in the 1930s in Irish American neighborhoods like Somerville, Charlestown, Dorchester, South Boston, and Roxbury.

James "Whitey" Bulger

James "Whitey" Bulger
Arrested in California

James "Whitey" Bulger was an old man when police finally caught him. After 16 years on the run, the 81-year-old mobster was ready to surrender. He had been on the FBI's Ten Most Wanted list for 12 years. A reward for information about Whitey and his girlfriend led to his arrest.

On June 22, 2011, Whitey was captured. He and his 60-year-old girlfriend, Catherine Greig, were living in Santa Monica, California. They'd been there since 1998. Police found $822,000 in cash, 30 loaded guns, and fake IDs in the apartment.

Whitey had been a powerful mob boss in Boston for a long time. He was said to have murdered 19 people. His crew was involved in organized crime activities.

Extortion was one of the ways Whitey's gang made money. They would tell people to pay, or get hurt. Loan sharking was another money maker. Gangsters loan people money at very high interest rates. Then if the people don't repay on time, they get hurt—or even killed.

Other crimes Whitey's gang was involved with included gambling, selling guns, and hijacking trucks at gunpoint. The criminals would then sell whatever goods the truck was hauling.

But Whitey was also known as a Robin Hood. He would go after drug dealers and protect the neighborhood people. He didn't allow heroin or PCP to be sold. And drug dealers who sold to kids were run out of town by Whitey's men.

Back in 1994, Whitey was about to be indicted on a charge of racketeering, or illegal business activities. But he never showed up. The day before he was to appear in court, he took off.

Later, it became known that Whitey had been an FBI informant. When other gangsters learned he had talked to the FBI, they wanted to get even. So they told the FBI about the 19 murders Whitey had committed.

When he disappeared right before his court date, police were suspicious. They were right to be. As it turned out, his FBI handler was corrupt. John J. Connolly, Jr., told Whitey he was about to be arrested. So Whitey left Boston immediately and went on the lam.

FBI Agent Connolly was later convicted of racketeering and second-degree murder.

During the 16 years before Whitey was caught, he lived a mostly quiet life. He and Catherine lived together in Santa Monica. Going by the names Charles and Carol Gasko, they kept to themselves.

Whitey's girlfriend was a cat lover. Through her kindness to an abandoned cat, Catherine met Anna Bjorn.

Tall and beautiful, Anna had been Miss Iceland in 1974. Her real last name was Bjornsdottir. But she shortened it to Bjorn when she came to America. Anna had earned $2,000 a day as a model for Noxzema. She had also acted in such movies as *More American Graffiti* and *The Sword and the Sorcerer.*

Anna lived in Iceland part of the year. The rest of the time she lived in Santa Monica. Her California home was near Whitey and Catherine.

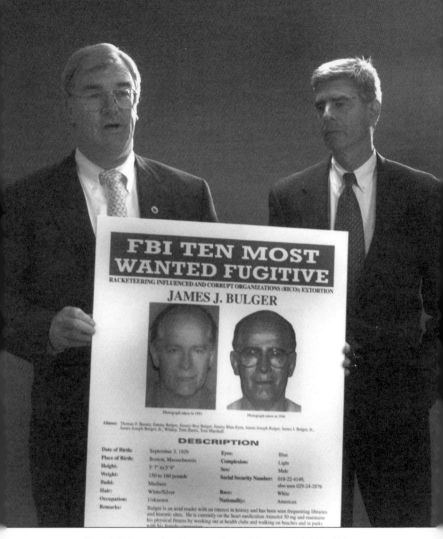

Special Agent in Charge Barry Mawn and US Attorney General Donald Stern hold a press conference naming Whitey Bulger to the FBI's Most Wanted List.

The two women got to know each other thanks to the abandoned cat. Catherine fed Tiger twice a day and took him to the vet when needed. So Anna knew Catherine well enough to remember her when a $100,000 reward was announced for Greig's capture.

On his 79th birthday, in 2008, the FBI had doubled the reward for capturing him to $2 million. Once Osama bin Laden was captured and killed, he was no longer number one on the Top 10 Most Wanted list. The agency's budget for finding Whitey went up. *America's Most Wanted* did episodes about Whitey. Police started showing daytime TV spots about Catherine. They were hoping to catch Whitey through her.

CNN covered the FBI's media blitz. That's how Anna Bjorn heard about it over in Iceland. She saw the spots on CNN and called the hotline. Later she got the $2 million reward. And that's how Whitey and Catherine were caught.

After 16 years, the manhunt was over. But it had been a long, hard road for the police. Whitey and Catherine had done a good job posing as Southern California retirees. Their neighbors thought they were just a nice old couple who valued their privacy.

"We were looking for a gangster," said a police detective. "But that was part of the problem. Whitey wasn't a gangster anymore."

One FBI agent said the manhunt was the most expensive in history. It cost millions of dollars to track down Whitey and Catherine.

Even though they avoided prison for 16 years, their life was not happy. Whitey lived in constant fear of being caught. He had to stay holed up inside the apartment, with black plastic taped to the windows.

These days Whitey is doing time at Plymouth County Correctional Facility in Massachusetts. He is 82 and in poor health. Catherine pleaded guilty to hiding Bulger, a known fugitive. She was sentenced to eight years in prison and fined $150,000.

GLOSSARY

autocrat—a ruler with supreme power

autopsy—an examination of a body after death to discover cause of death

Avengers—a group that hunts Nazi criminals and brings them to justice

Baath—a political party in Iraq

boarding school—a place where students live while they attend school

commercial plane—aircraft used to carry cargo or passengers for payment

compound—an area enclosed by a fence

concentration camp—a Nazi prison where many people were tortured and killed; death camp

coup—a sudden attack to take over a government

demagogue—a leader who sways people with emotion

free state—a state that outlawed slavery

frenzy—great panic or excitement; madness

fugitive—someone who is running away

Gestapo—the German secret police

ghetto—a part of a city where a minority group is forced to live

hostage—someone taken by force or pressure by someone else

hostiles—a term used long ago to identify groups of Native Americans who resisted government orders

inmate—a prisoner

Kurds—an ethnic group living in northern Iraq

loan shark—a moneylender who charges extremely high interest rates

manhunt—an organized search for a person, especially a criminal

master—in the old South, the boss of slaves

Mossad—an Israeli spy group

organized crime—a group of professional criminals who rely on crime as a way of life

peasant—a poor farmer or worker

privilege—a favor that is granted to someone

regime—a government

safe house—a secret hiding place

Shiites—a religious group in Iraq; a member of a branch of Islam

slave—a person made to work against his or her will; a person who is owned by another

slave state—a state that allowed slavery

sniper—someone who hides and shoots at others

talons—claws, especially belonging to a bird of prey

trident—three-pronged spear

tarot card—a card used to tell fortunes

vent—an opening for air

warden—the person in charge of a prison

witness—someone who sees something take place

wound—to injure

Index